These are the **Great** Falls at Clon. Here, the waters of the **Blood** River fall fifty feet, into Dead Man Creek.

It is a **dangerous** place. The water rolls over the **rocks** like angry white horses. You can see bits of old boats **between** the rocks. Black birds **fly** over them.
But it is a very beautiful place.

1

There is one boat which lies **quietly** at the side of the Creek. The waters of the Creek go **past** it. The boat's windows are always open. Fitzwilliam Brown and his wife Lulu like **fresh air**.

It is a **warm** day today. Lulu Brown is sitting on one side of the boat and writing something. She **moves** back and looks at her work. It looks nice. DEAD MAN TOURIST OFFICE, CLON, it says.

'Is that all right?' she asks her husband.

But Fitzwilliam Brown does not answer. He is already walking up the hill to the Falls. After today, Fitzwilliam will be a rich man.

Behind the Falls there runs a **narrow** line of rock. If you walk along it, you'll see a big black hole. Here Dead Man Caves **begin**. And Fitzwilliam has bought the Caves.

From tomorrow, it will cost you fifty cents if you go into the Caves. . . . Fitz puts his hand on the gate. He opens it. He shuts it. Opens it again. That's all right. He goes in.

He moves the switches of the lights in the **first** cave. That's O.K. In the **second** cave. That's all right. 'Aha! Satan's Cave is next!' He moves the switch. **No** lights!

'Something's **wrong**!' he says to **himself**. His own **voice** makes him afraid. He goes back quickly. 'I'll have to **get** a new switch. All the **visitors** will be here tomorrow.' He leaves the Caves.

Below him, the water of the Great Falls rolls with a great noise into the Creek. From there, it slips angrily between the rocks, between the trees, into the great green Moon River.

On many days, you don't see any thing on the Moon River. But today, far away, you'll see a boat. As it comes nearer, you'll see a big man in it. As the boat moves quietly along, he **watches** the trees.

t is Ted **Beard**, an ugly man and one of the Beautiful Boys of Bly Street. He's just come from prison. Five years he's been there. The **eason?** The 20,000 dollar robbery rom the Bristol **Bank** in 197-.

Ted has come for the money. The Boys are waiting, and he has to find it. Ted takes out his map. DEAD MAN CREEK, it says. He looks over the river. 'That's it!' He laughs to himself.

Quickly he **stops** the large boat and **climbs** into the small boat behind it. He moves across the river. As the boat rides quietly into the Creek, Ted's mouth opens in **surprise.**

'A boat! **Perhaps** they've found our money! The Boys will kill me!' He can't take his eyes from the other boat. As he watches it, a woman comes out and walks away, between the trees.

Ted thinks hard for a **moment**. Then, before the Blood River can **carry** him back into the Moon River, he moves. He **pulls** the boat to the side of the Creek, and hides it in the tall **grass.**

He jumps out and runs nearer the Falls. He hides behind a tree. As he **reaches** it, a man walks out from behind the Falls. He goes down to the boat. His face is hard and angry.

'Fitz!'
A voice behind him. Ted nearly
falls into the Creek. It's that
woman from the boat.
'Fitz! I'm over here!'
The woman **must** be in the grass.

'Where are my switches?' comes the
man's voice. He goes into the boat.
'She hasn't seen me,' thinks Ted.
He **stands** there as quiet as a **mouse.**
The woman comes out of the grass
and calls to the man.

'Fitz, we've done **enough** work this
morning,' she calls. '**Let's rest**
for a bit.' She goes into the boat.
'Now's the time,' thinks Ted. And
he runs quickly past the boat.

He reaches the top of the hill, by the Falls. He **turns** and looks back. 'They haven't seen me!' His eyes return to the Falls. He walks along the narrow line of rock behind them.

Suddenly there's a tall gate in front of him. He can't get past! He looks down. Thirty feet below, the angry, white water. He shuts his eyes. **Only** one way in. . . .

His hands **hold** the gate like a very dear friend. **Slowly,** he moves **around** it. Time stands still. . . . His feet are slipping. The noise of the Falls fills his ears.
'I'm falling!' he thinks . . . .

He throws himself into the mouth of the cave. For two **minutes** he rests on the **wet ground.** Then he **gets up** and takes out his map. He **points** his light around the cave.

'It's all different! This isn't the same cave!' He rubs his eyes and looks at the map again. It must be the same cave. But it's full of lights . . . and chairs . . . and THIS WAY PLEASE . . . and everything!

What's the next cave like? Another gate. This time it's a small one. He climbs the gate. On the other side, his foot slips. His hand catches something in the **darkness.** A switch. . . . 'Aaaaaaahhhh!!'

In the darkness, the face of Satan **laughs at** him.
'I don't **feel well**!' Ted turns and climbs the gate again. As his foot comes over the gate, it hits the switch.

Satan's face isn't there any more. 'It was only some rocks in the light!' He laughs to himself. His voice rings out in the darkness. . . . Two caves later, he looks at the map. 'This is the **right** cave.'

On one side, a **heap** of rocks. The money's **under** there! He pulls back the rocks. It isn't! It must be the wrong place. Ted looks here. And there. And there. . . . Footsteps! Someone's coming!

He throws the rocks back on the
heap. One big rock is too **heavy**.
He leaves it, and runs into the
darkness. The footsteps reach
the next cave.

Ted can **almost** see the man's **shape**.
A voice from the next cave: 'Now
where have I put my pen**knife**?'
A lamp points into the darkness
over Ted's head.
'It must be in the boat.'

The footsteps return to the mouth
of the Caves.
Ted gets up and rubs the **dust** from
his clothes. He takes a step. As
he moves, his feet slip under him.
He falls into a black hole.

As he falls, his hands catch the earth and rock and other things in the sides of the hole. 'I'm falling to the other side of the world,' he **feels.** And it hurts.

He opens his eyes, slowly. Over his head he sees the **leaves** of a tree. A lot of trees. He's in a **forest.** He looks at his hand. Yes, there's blood on it. But that's not all.

He opens his hand. Paper. Money. Paper money. Ten dollars. A lot of ten dollars. Hundreds of dollars. He looks back, and sees a hole in the rocks. The money's in the hole! He laughs and laughs.

Hahahaha! hohohoho! 'It's in the hole!' He throws it up in the air. 'Can I help you?' Someone is standing over him. He sits up. It's the girl from the boat. Why is she here?

What does she want? She wants his money! He **covers** it with his body. He says, 'It's all right. I'm not hurt. I'm all right.' He **pushes** her away.

She watches him as he goes. He holds the money to his body. What a **strange** man, she thinks. Does he live near here? He'll fall into the marsh if he's not **careful**. She waits and **listens**. . . .

Help! Ted's feet are in the marsh and he's falling **deeper** into it. 'Fitz! Come and help! There's a man in the marsh!' **Both** of them run to help Ted.

'Quick! Bring some **sticks**,' calls Fitz. 'Put them across **each other**, like this.' Ted's legs are deep in the marsh. His hands reach for the sticks, but they are too short. Lulu runs to get longer sticks.

At last Ted's hands catch a stick. **Together**, Fitz and Lulu pull and pull. Ted climbs out of the marsh. And, **without** a 'thank you', he pushes past them and runs away into the wood.

14

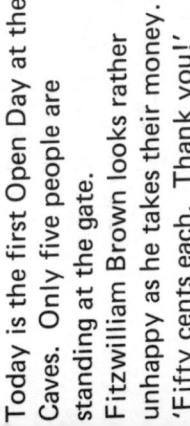

Today is the first Open Day at the Caves. Only five people are standing at the gate. Fitzwilliam Brown looks rather unhappy as he takes their money. 'Fifty cents each. Thank you!'

Inside the Caves, Lulu shows everyone around. But she doesn't always **remember** the right names. 'And this, **ladies and gentlemen,** is the Great Grey Cave!' She moves the switch.

What a surprise! The five visitors see a small cave with **yellow** rocks. A very small, very yellow cave. 'And that,' says a tall man, 'is the WAY IN!' He points to the WAY OUT. Everyone laughs.

At five o'clock, Fitz **closes** the gate. For more **than** an hour now, **nobody** has come.
Lulu comes over to him. 'Don't be too unhappy,' she says. 'Tomorrow will be **better.'**

Fitz's face gets longer every minute. 'It's all been a great **mistake,** Lulu. Who's going to come tomorrow? Nobody, that's who.'
Lulu asks, 'Shall I turn on the floodlights? It's getting dark.'

'No,' says Fitz with a long face, 'nobody is watching.'
As he says this, there is the **sound** of steps behind him. A young woman comes to the gate.
'Who are you?' he asks her.

'I'm a reporter,' says the young woman. 'I'm from *The Sun.* I've just met my friend Harry. He's just visited your Caves. There's something strange here, he says. Holes in the ground. Things move.'

'What's that?' asks Fitz quickly. The woman's **silly.** 'Holes? Things that move? **Not true** at all! My Caves are very **safe.** Please don't say anything like that about my Caves. And please leave at once.'

The next day, Fitz is sitting quietly over his breakfast. 'Anyone waiting at the gate?' he asks. When Lulu says nothing, he opens his **newspaper.** His face turns white. 'Lulu! Listen to this!'

'WHAT'S **HAPPENING** AT CLON CAVES? Is something wrong at Dead Man Creek? Visitors have seen great holes in the Caves. The ground moves under their feet. Is there an **animal** living in Dead Man Caves?'

'It's that reporter!' says Lulu. 'Let's close the Caves today,' says Fitz. 'Put on the gate: NO VISITORS TODAY. I'm going **round** all the Caves. It's not true. I've never seen any animals there at all.'

Fitz turns on all the lights. He and Lulu look together. At one **end** they find a man's shoe. It's not Fitz's. Then a box. 'Someone's been here!' cries Lulu. 'Sshh! What's that noise?' says Fitz.

He runs to the mouth of the Caves. Twenty-five or more people are waiting at the gate. At the sides of the Creek, six or seven large boats are bringing hundreds more. It looks like a festival!

'**Let** us in! We want the Monster!' says one woman. 'Yes! Where is it?' cries another. Fitz pushes them back. 'There's no monster here!' But the woman is **stronger**. She pushes in, and the others **follow**.

The money rolls into Fitz's hand as they **pass**. The last person stops. Her hand rests on Fitz's. He looks up. It's the woman reporter. 'I'm going to look for the holes. Remember?' She **smiles sweetly**.

Inside the Caves there is chaos, with people everywhere. They push sticks into the ground. They look behind rocks. They make noises like dogs. They cry like cats. 'Where's the Monster?' asks a woman happily.

The woman reporter hides in a **dark** place and watches. After a time, she sees a dark shape in a cave to the side. But just then, a woman walks in front of her and goes into the cave. . . .

'Aaaahhh!' The woman's voice hits the **roof.**
'The Thing! The Thing! It's in there!'
She runs out of the cave as **fast** as her legs will carry her.

The next day, *The Sunday Sun* says: MONSTER IN CLON CAVES! ARE THE CAVES SAFE? Fitz's face turns red when he sees it. 'It's not true!' he cries. Lulu pulls a long face.

But that afternoon she comes out of the boat, and her face changes. Hundreds of people are standing at the gate. Boats are **arriving** with **more and more.** A man is selling ALL ABOUT THE MONSTER.

All **week**, things have been good for the Browns. They have bought a Son et Lumière, and tonight — Friday — will be its first night. On all the boats in the Creek, everyone is waiting for the lights. Lights!

Suddenly it **seems** like day at the Falls. **Music** from *The Valkyrie* fills the Creek. And, **high** on the narrow rocks by the Falls, the floodlights catch three small shapes. They are carrying heavy boxes.

At first, they stand like stones. They've come out of the wrong hole! Lulu says: 'Fitz! The one in front! It's that man with the beard.' At her side, a voice says: 'Yes. It's the Beautiful Boys!'

Lulu doesn't hear. But Ted seems to hear. He throws his box into the Creek. The water **dances** angrily and carries it away. Ted puts his hand to his eyes; then he turns, and runs behind the Falls. Everyone laughs.

'That's a good trick,' says a voice.
'Yes. Who are they?' asks another.
'I don't know. Perhaps they're all
monsters!' says another. Everyone
laughs again. This is a **fine** Son et
Lumière!

Behind the Falls, the gate stands
between the Caves and the Boys. And
it won't open! 'Push it!' cries an
old Boy. The man in front runs at
it. He hits it. Nothing happens. He
tries again; the others help.

Fitz and his friends are running up
the hill. Ted can hear their feet.
He turns to Bert Beautiful.
'Quick! You try!'
Bert runs at the gate like a bus.
It opens, and Bert falls **off**.

23

Down he falls, into the Creek.
Everyone laughs. Another fine
trick!
The other Boys run into the Caves.
One minute later, Fitz and his men
arrive. The Boys have gone!

Fitz runs into the Caves. Chairs
are lying on the **floor.** Someone
has pulled rocks **against** the
way in to the Caves.
'That way!' cries Fitz. 'They've
gone into the caves at the back!'

He and his men pull the rocks from
the door.
Suddenly everything goes dark. Ted
and the Boys have found the switch!
In the darkness, Fitz can see only
his **watch.** Twelve o'clock!

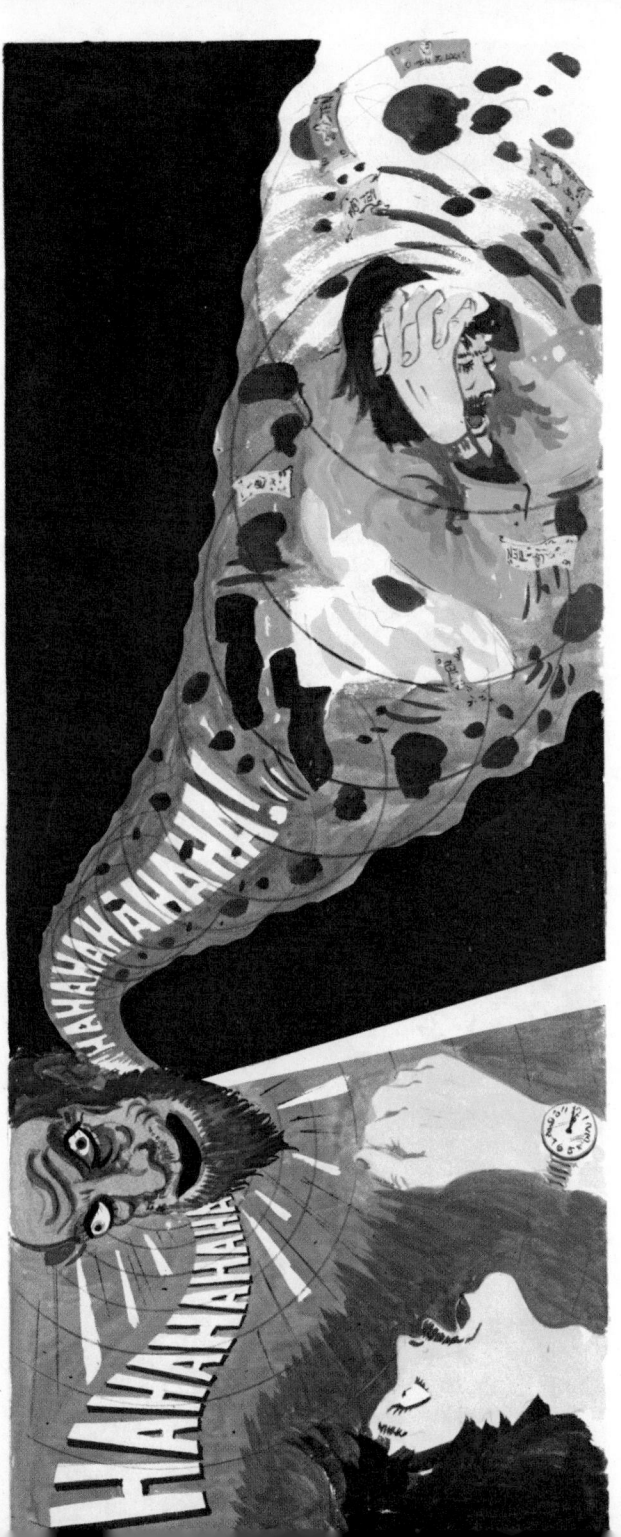

Hahahahaha! He looks up. Over him, the face of Satan laughs and laughs. Ted has found all the switches! Fitz calls: 'Go back, men. I'm going to look for the other switch.'

He takes **several** steps out of the cave. Just then, the ground under his feet becomes **soft**. It's earth! It's a hole! A large one! His feet slip under him.

Hahahaha! The voice of Satan again. Fitz falls into the hole. And rolls, down and down. He feels **sick**. Is there no end to the hole?

Suddenly he is outside again, in the night. He can see the lights of the Son et Lumière behind the hill. He gets up and rubs the dust from his clothes. In the darkness, the dust feels like paper.

He holds his coat to the **half**-light. It's not dust. It's paper! But no. It's. . . not paper, it's. . . money! 'My money!' thinks Fitz. 'They've been in my Caves. They've taken my money! The monsters!'

'Robbery!' he says **loudly**. 'If the money's from my Caves, it's my money. I'll catch them. You'll see!' Just then, he sees the shape of a man in the darkness. Is the man going to the hole?

'That's one of them,' says Fitz to himself. He hides behind a tree, although it is quite dark. 'This time, I'll take something from him,' thinks Fitz.

The man comes nearer. Fitz throws himself at the dark shape. Fitz is a heavy person, and the strange man falls under him. They **fight**. At last Fitz gets on top, and hits the other man on the head.

Fitz looks in the man's coat, and finds a dusty letter. He holds it to the half-light, and reads slowly: 'Boys! Don't work tonight. Leave the money **until** tomorrow. There's a festival at the Falls. I.Q.'

'Robbery! I'll catch them. You'll see!' says Fitz to the darkness. He runs for his **helpers**; he has had an idea. He reaches the Falls. 'You two: go to the gate with four others. You others, come with me!'

They go back to the hole **among** the trees. 'Bring wood. We're going to make a fire. The smoke will go up the hole and fill the Caves. They'll have to come out through the gate.'

The fire gets bigger and bigger. Fitz throws wet grass on it. The smoke gets **thicker.** People come and watch. But, at the gate, there is no sound from the Caves. Perhaps the men have gone. Or what?

Out in front of the Falls,
everyone is watching the Son et
Lumière still. It's a quiet part:
the music is soft; the lights are
low. It's the romantic bit.
Fitz runs to the front of the hill.

He looks up. Is someone moving
behind the Falls? 'Lights!' he calls.
'Ssshhh!' cries a voice.
Fitz runs up the hill.
'Ssshhh,' call many voices. 'Stop
that man!' But Fitz has gone.

And suddenly all the lights are **on
fire.** There is an angry cry from
the people who are watching. But
just then, they see something at
the mouth of the Caves. Three **tired**
men. Three black men.

It is Ted and his men. Their clothes and faces are black with smoke. Ted's beard is almost blacker than Satan's. He tries to **use** his feet, but they won't carry him. He slips, and falls into the Creek.

He **swims** in the water. Then a small boat reaches him, and a man pulls him out of the water. In the boat, the man says sadly to Ted: 'You're not a Beautiful Boy at all, Ted.' It is a man from the Bristol Bank.

'I've waited a long time for you, Ted,' he says. 'Now you've shown me where the money is. It's there, in the Caves, isn't it?' The water runs from Ted's hair. It runs from his eyes. 'Yes,' he says.

A year later, there are two boats on Dead Man Creek. A big, rich one – the Browns' – and a smaller one. On the side of the smaller one it says: TED BEARD, INC.

Up at the Falls, outside the gate, there is a long line of people. SEE THE CAVES. 75 CENTS EACH. SEE SATAN'S CAVE. SATAN HIMSELF WILL BE THERE FROM TEN UNTIL FIVE, says a large notice.

Inside Satan's Cave, Ted is feeling quite tired. It's been a long, hard day. He has to laugh all day. Satan's work isn't easy. He holds out his hand. 'Thank you.' Money isn't everything, he thinks.

Topic words

Questions

1. Say everything you know about Dead Man Creek and the Great Falls at Clon. If you can, draw a map.
2. Who do Dead Man Caves belong to?
3. Why has Ted Beard come to Dead Man Creek? Has he been here before?
4. Why does Ted's mouth open in surprise?
5. Say what happens after Ted gets into the small boat.
6. What happens to Ted when he arrives in the Caves?
7. What is the earth like in the Caves? Why are there holes in the ground?
8. Where is the money? Who finds it? Where? When?
9. Where does Lulu see Ted for the first time? Where does she see him for the second time?
10. Who helps Ted out of the marsh? What with?
11. Why does *The Sunday Sun* say: 'Monster in Clon Caves'? Why does the reporter think this?
12. What happens on Sunday afternoon?
13. Whose shoe do Fitz and Lulu find? (page 18)
14. Why does the woman (page 20) run out of the cave?
15. Why does Ted throw his box into the Creek?
16. What do the *visitors* think when they see him?
17. Where does Fitz fall?
18. Who is the man at the Son et Lumière who knows the Beautiful Boys?
19. How does Fitz get the Beautiful Boys out of the Caves?
20. What work does Ted do later?